Character
Education

Controversial Issues in Education

Tracking: Conflicts and Resolutions
Character Education: Controversy and Consensus
Debating National Standards
Gender Equity in Schools
Gifted and Talented Education
Inclusion Issues for Schools
Interdisciplinary Curriculum

Character Education

Controversy and Consensus

Anne Turnbaugh Lockwood

CORWIN PRESS, INC.
A Sage Publications Company
Thousand Oaks, California

For information:

Corwin Press, Inc.
A Sage Publications Company
2455 Teller Road
Thousand Oaks, California 91320
E-mail: order@corwin.sagepub.com

SAGE Publications Ltd.
6 Bonhill Street
London EC2A 4PU
United Kingdom

SAGE Publications India Pvt. Ltd.
M-32 Market
Greater Kailash I
New Delhi 110 048 India

Printed in the United States of America

Library of Congress Cataloging-in-Publication Data

Lockwood, Anne Turnbaugh.
    Character education: controversy and consensus / Anne
Turnbaugh Lockwood.
        p. cm. — (Controversial issues in education)
    Includes bibliographical references.
    ISBN 0-8039-6584-2 (pbk. : acid-free paper). — ISBN 0-8039-6616-4
(cloth : acid-free paper)
        1. Moral education — United States.   I. Title.   II. Series.
    LC311.L57   1997
    370.11'4—dc21   97-4904

This book is printed on acid-free paper.

97 98 99 00 01 02 03 10 9 8 7 6 5 4 3 2 1

Production Editor: S. Marlene Head
Editorial Assistant: Kristen L. Gibson
Typesetters: William C. E. Lawrie and Laura A. Lawrie
Cover Designer: Marcia R. Finlayson

Contents

Acknowledgments   vii

About the Author   viii

Introduction: Why Character Education?   1

• What the Reader Will Discover • What Is Character
Education? • Consensus on Character Education's
Meaning • Values Clarification and Its Legacy • Moral
Dilemmas and Lawrence Kohlberg • Selected Goals
for Current Character Education • Criticisms of
Character Education

1. Character Education and the Hard Business of
Schooling: Kevin Ryan   12

• Psychology Versus the Development of Character
• Evaluating Character Education • Parenting and
Character • The Character Education Manifesto: An
Agenda for Action • The Study of Virtue

2. The Current Condition of Character Education:
James S. Leming   22

• The Diversity of Current Programs • Why Character
Education? • Elementary Versus Secondary Programs
• The Volatility of Character Education Programs

• The Role of Parent Participation • Assessing Character Education

3. Character Education and Its Prospects for Success: James R. Rest   31

   • The Evidence: Values and Behavior • The Need for Research • What Is Character Education?

4. Character Education in the Classroom: Phyllis Smith-Hansen   38

   • Character Education and Teachers • Moral Education's Demise and Current Character Education • Discussions of Moral Dilemmas • Character Education and Teaching • A Classroom Suffused With Character • Character Education and Reflective Practice

5. A Grassroots Character Education Program: Deborah Linden   48

   • The Development of a Grassroots Program • Outcomes of Character Education • Implementing Character Education: One Program's Process • Schoolwide Character Education • Evaluating Character Education • Is Character Education the Answer?

6. Schoolwide Character Education: James Antis   60

   • The Choice of Materials • The Volatility of Character Education • Desired Outcomes • Implementing Character Education • Effectiveness of Character Education: One Study

References and Selected Bibliography   69

   • References • Selected Bibliography

Acknowledgments

This overview of discussion about the controversial topic of character education—along with actual experiences of school staff working with programs—could not have been undertaken without the cooperation of the individuals featured in this volume. I thank each person for his or her unique contribution.

Recommendations of practitioners to feature in this volume came from Professor James Leming and the Center for the 4th and 5th Rs at the State University of New York–Cortland. I sincerely appreciate their help in identifying individuals who could speak about their experiences in schools related specifically to character education.

I wish to thank Alice Foster and Marlene Head at Corwin Press for first taking on this series and then equipping the endeavor with considerable production expertise.

Finally, although I always thank my husband, Alan L. Lockwood, I especially appreciate his counsel on this topic.

ANNE TURNBAUGH LOCKWOOD

About the Author

Anne Turnbaugh Lockwood, an education writer and analyst, is an Honorary Fellow in the Department of Curriculum and Instruction at the University of Wisconsin–Madison. Her work focuses on diminishing the barriers between research and practice. She is the author of numerous reports, articles, and other publications for the U.S. Department of Education's North Central Regional Educational Laboratory, the Hispanic Dropout Project, the Office of Bilingual Education and Minority Language Affairs, and the Office of Educational Research and Improvement. At the University of Wisconsin, she developed two nationally respected programs of publications for the National Center on Effective Secondary Schools and the National Center for Effective Schools, respectively. Her work has been recognized by the American Educational Research Association Interpretive Scholarship Award and by the University of Wisconsin's School of Education. She is also the author of *Conversations With Educational Leaders: Contemporary Viewpoints on Education in America* (State University of New York Press, 1997) and *Tracking: Conflicts and Resolutions* (Corwin Press, 1996).

Introduction: Why Character Education?

When the topic of character education comes up for discussion, as it frequently does in educational circles in the late 1990s, confusion is a common consequence. Proponents of character education make their case forcefully, insisting that teaching virtue and values in public schools will lead to the betterment of behavior and society as a whole. Those without much direct knowledge of character education, its goals, and its applications may find these arguments persuasive but still believe that character education is an elusive concept. In fact, the prospective student of character education—or the educator in search of an effective program—easily can be overwhelmed by the sheer diversity of curricula, institutions, books, and other materials that all hold claim to the rather nebulous territory known as character education.

A brief Internet tour amply illustrates this confusion and diversity. One site, known as The Character Education Page, provides a menu complete with hyperlinked text that includes the following:

- A general introduction to character education
- Institutions with an interest in character education
- Non-Internet resources
- Internet resources devoted to character education

- Internet resources for religious education
- Educators with an interest in character education
- Resources related to the philosophy of character and virtue
- Miscellaneous links that might be of interest (Cunningham, 1997)

As this menu suggests, character education can overlap with religion, philosophy, ethics, or citizenship. A brief look at the institutions listed on the menu again demonstrates the diversity that all seems to fit under the generous umbrella of character education. For example, one institution listed is the Institute for Global Ethics, described as "an independent, nonsectarian, and nonpolitical organization dedicated to elevating public awareness and promoting the discussion of ethics in a global context"(Cunningham, 1997). Another, the Character Education Institute in San Antonio, Texas, describes its mission as one that helps "children develop into responsible citizens by serving as the leading recognized educational foundation devoted to the development, distribution, and implementation of the Character Education Curriculum in elementary, middle, and high schools throughout the world" (Cunningham, 1997).

Still other organizations linked to this site include Project No-Spank, which, as the name suggests, disavows physical punishment. The Separation of School and State Alliance also is included as a character education organization, although its members believe that public schools cannot and should not attempt to teach values.

The "miscellaneous links" portion of the menu includes a "Character Quote of the Week" from a school guidance counselor in Randolph County, North Carolina; the M. K. Gandhi Institute for Nonviolence; the Carl Gustav Jung Center of Houston, Texas; and "Ethics Updates" for ethics instructors and students.

Obviously, a plethora of approaches, some with conflicting goals, are synonymous with any consideration of current character education. In partial response to the confusion, and also as a means of highlighting central, broad themes and consensus about character education, the purpose of this monograph is focused and limited. Its goal is to provide students and educators interested in learning more about character education with a primer that outlines, discusses, and critiques the key issues surrounding the topic.

Why write a book on character education? Although many do not know what character education is, it has attained a position of prominence on the national educational agenda. President Clinton called for a return to teaching values in public schools in his 1996 State of the Union Address, saying, "I challenge all our schools to teach character education, to teach good values and good citizenship." The Association for Supervision and Curriculum Development formed a Task Force on Character Education. Other national associations, such as the National Council for the Social Studies, are following suit with their own position statements on character education. One White House conference on character education has been convened; another is planned as this book goes to press. Several states are adopting legislation that will mandate character education programs in public schools. Clearly, character education has become an educational powerhouse that should be understood by both the student of education and the educator who may wish to enact a program of character education.

What the Reader Will Discover

To shed light on a topic that seems crystal clear to its advocates but murky to those outside its thrall, I chose six individuals from research and practice to interview in a series of conversations presented in this volume. These conversations are supplemented with a selected bibliography.

Three individuals featured in this volume are nationally recognized authorities with expertise in the fields of character education and moral development. I chose these particular individuals on the basis of their reputations, their writings and/or research, and in two cases, prior interviews with me. These individuals, through responses to my questions, examine and critique the current character movement.

Three others are practitioners—each with a distinct approach to character education—who speak to the practical side of designing, implementing, and evaluating character education. These practitioners were recommended to me by James S. Leming, who is featured in this book, and by the Center for the 4th and 5th Rs, directed by Thomas Lickona, another leader in the national character education movement.

All interviews were conducted by telephone and were tape-recorded. After reviewing the transcript of each interview, I wrote my drafts, which I then sent to each interviewee. This gave each individual the opportunity to read the segment containing his or her comments and make suggestions for changes. These changes were then incorporated into the final version of the manuscript.

I identified central, key questions culled from my own search of the literature, scrutiny of character education curricula and programs, and previous writing on the topic (Lockwood, 1994, 1997). These questions include, but are not limited to, the following: What is character education? What do character educators hope to accomplish? Does character education "work"? What evidence do we need in order to assess its success or failure? What does contemporary character education look like in action? Will parents and community members know it when they see it—just as they would recognize mathematics, social studies, or creative writing if they stepped into their children's classrooms? Finally, what criticisms can be leveled against character education in its most recent incarnation?

What Is Character Education?

Part of the confusion associated with current character education efforts stems from the lack of a universal definition of character education. In part, this may be a result of most character educators' rejection of the recent past and other attempts to teach values in the public schools.

In the 1920s, a concerted and deliberate effort to focus on issues related to good character took root in American schools, prompted by concerns about the erosion of society—concerns very similar to those held by character educators today. But the results of large-scale research and evaluation undertaken by Hugh Hartshorne, Mark A. May, and associates (1927), found that despite these educative efforts, values did not predict individuals' choice of behavior in a real-life situation. In other words, individuals' actual behavior remained situational no matter how they had been schooled about values. This key and central finding ran counter to what the researchers wanted to discover, but it sounded a death knell for character education in the public schools in any purposeful sense for many years.

In the 1960s and 1970s, educators talked of "moral education" and the acquisition of "values." Current character education advocates deliberately choose different terms to describe their efforts and goals—quite possibly because they have distanced themselves from what they perceive as ill-conceived efforts to develop moral reasoning or clarify values in youth. As a result, they have settled on the term *character education* as the semantic vehicle to carry their aspirations.

Current character education advocates emphasize the development of "virtue," "life skills," "citizenship skills," and so on. The word *values* is usually avoided, because character educators are sensitive to the possibility for political dissension within schools, districts, and communities when this term is introduced. They have learned that when people discuss values, the question of whose values should be taught often emerges and can lead either to unwelcome public controversy or to a premature demise for a fledgling program.

What is character education in its current form? Oddly, no standard definition prevails. As the examples in this book reveal, educators engaged in character education may do very different things. They may emphasize a discrete set of skills; claim a focus on citizenship; or, more largely, define character education as everything that takes place in a classroom or school. They may focus primarily on school climate and environment or drill students on lists of character attributes; the lists themselves can vary from the very brief to the lengthy.

Alan L. Lockwood (1997), in an article that points to the critical need for a definition of character education, proposes a working definition that he synthesizes from the literature of character educators themselves: "Character education is defined as any school-initiated program, designed in cooperation with other community institutions, to shape directly and systematically the behavior of young people by influencing explicitly the nonrelativistic values believed directly to bring about that behavior" (p. 6).

Agreeing upon a focused meaning of character education is especially critical as schools, states, and professional organizations buy into the character education agenda, invest resources into character education curricula and training, and struggle to implement a program. A common definition would also aid prospective researchers and program evaluators seeking demonstrable evidence of the effectiveness of character education in order to justify its existence, refine their existing efforts, or drop their program in favor of a different educative effort.

Consensus on Character Education's Meaning

Character educators, who debate freely many aspects of character education, do appear to agree on two fundamental goals and beliefs: (a) Influencing youths' values in a prosocial direction will result in good, prosocial behavior; and (b) ethical relativism is unacceptable.

The connection that current character educators draw between values and behavior is the core of the contemporary character education movement, but whether this connection can withstand empirical tests is hotly debated, as demonstrated later in this volume. Certainly, as stated earlier, the classic set of empirical studies that measured the relationship between values and behavior failed to find a correlation (Hartshorne & May, 1927).

Proponents of character education advance their cause by pointing to the disarray of contemporary American society, random acts of violence, urban terror, and high rates of drug and alcohol abuse. They argue that something must be done to rectify this situation and redeem American youth. That something, they believe, is the inculcation of values, taught in a deliberate, authoritative way to youth in public schools with plenty of parental and community involvement.

Although character education's goals do include maintaining a determined grip on prosocial, good behavior, they also are nebulous and far-ranging. They include both relatively modest and immensely ambitious aspirations. These goals range from everyday "niceness" to nothing less than the overhaul of contemporary American society. As they argue for a focus on positive values and good behavior, character educators frequently refer *negatively* to Values Clarification, Lawrence Kohlberg, the moral dilemma discussion approach, or the moral reasoning approach; these terms are often used interchangeably. To what do these terms refer, and why are they relevant to current character education?

Values Clarification and Its Legacy

Values Clarification was a program that achieved considerable popularity in the 1970s. Its primary purpose was to assist students in the choice of values that would then guide their actions. Proponents of Values Clarification believed that the society of the time made it difficult for people to be clear about their values; they intended their program to help students clarify their values. A central belief of Values Clarification was that until people obtain values, they cannot meet the desired outcomes of Values Clarification, namely, overcoming confusion and acquiring a sense of purpose.

An integral part of the Values Clarification approach was a set of criteria used to determine whether a belief was indeed a value. In order to be a value, it had to be

- Chosen freely
- Chosen from alternatives
- Chosen after careful consideration of the consequences of each alternative
- Prized or cherished
- Publicly affirmed
- Acted upon
- Acted upon regularly (Raths, Harmin, & Simon, 1966, pp. 28-30)

In classrooms using Values Clarification techniques, teachers were encouraged to establish a nonjudgmental atmosphere and to respond to student views with "clarifying responses," which asked students to apply the seven criteria above to their own beliefs and behaviors. Examples of clarifying responses include the following: "Where did you get that idea?" "Did you consider other choices?" "What would be the consequences of these choices?" "Are you willing to put money behind that idea?" "Do you do this often?" (Raths et al., 1966, pp. 63-65).

Why is Values Clarification important? Current character educators reject Values Clarification as an egregious example of all that is wrong with both contemporary society and schooling. In Values Clarification, because a value is essentially neutral, there is no clear right or wrong judgment placed upon a student's choice. Ethical relativism reigns. Character educators argue that this approach to teaching values does not lend itself to furthering prosocial, "good" behavior. Instead, they assert that Values Clarification legitimizes any value a student might choose as long as the student can provide reasons to support his or her choice.

Moral Dilemmas and Lawrence Kohlberg

The moral reasoning approach is variously known as "Kohlberg's approach," "the dilemmas discussion approach," the "moral reasoning approach," or some combination of these terms. Lawrence Kohlberg was a Harvard-based psychologist who became famous for his research on the development of moral judgment. This research led to the identification of six stages of moral reasoning, which develop separately and sequentially. Higher stages—which, for various reasons, all individuals will not attain—are considered to represent more defensible forms of moral reasoning.

In its application in school settings, the moral reasoning/moral development approach is carried out through a series of dilemma discussions that are led by the teacher. In a typical exercise, the teacher matches students exhibiting one stage of reasoning with students using a higher stage of reasoning. In another common manifestation of the dilemma discussion approach, the teacher either uses small groups in which students debate their reasons with others or else leads a class discussion (Lockwood, 1976). Values Clarification and the moral development approach are often viewed synonymously by current character educators, but they are quite different and distinct. Most character educators object to the moral development approach just as strenuously as they do to Values Clarification. They point to its use of moral dilemma discussions and claim that these dilemmas are artificial, contrived, and ultimately useless. Because students are encouraged to reason through situations that present moral choices and dilemmas, character educators believe that these dilemma discussions promote ethical relativism. In fact, many current character educators point to both the Values Clarification approach and the moral reasoning approach as iron-clad reasons why moral education failed in the 1960s and 1970s.

Selected Goals for Current Character Education

Although goals of the current character education movement vary in both size and scope, it is safe to assert that contemporary character educators unite against ethical relativism. No matter which approach or activity is used to further character education, these educators believe that there is a concrete, tangible, and discrete set of right and wrong values and behaviors. They also stand firm on the correlation between good values and prosocial behavior, although to date there is no research that firmly establishes such a correlation. Current character educators also maintain that the Values Clarification approach and the moral reasoning approach, although quite dissimilar, can promote both moral confusion and rationalization of bad behavior.

The most dramatic goals for character education include restoring American society to a time when crime was rare, communities were tightly knit, families were intact, and prosocial behavior was the norm. However, character educators appear to ignore other contributing factors to the condition of society. They rarely discuss the culture of poverty, the effects of corporate downsizing on the middle class, the fiscal constraints of public schools and social service agencies, or the increased polarization of classes and ethnic and racial groups within American society. They do discuss dissolution of the two-parent family, the demise of traditional values, and a general lack of discipline as contributing to society's current condition. In short, character educators maintain a traditional focus that insists on a restoration of an orderly American past. This restoration takes a "pull yourself up by your bootstraps" approach to the business of acquiring virtue, getting a good education, and succeeding in life and society.

More limited goals for character education focus on the teacher, others on the classroom and school climate, and still others on desired parenting practices, but all share one common denominator: *They seek to change youth behavior on both an everyday scale—transforming everyday, casual rudeness to polite conduct—and a larger scale—seeing youth choose prosocial, "moral" behavior, no matter what the situation.* Below, I list selected, more modest goals expressed by character educators.

- Character educators want schools to be more pleasant places for both adults and students.
- Character educators would like to see the teacher regain a sort of authority in the classroom that they believe has been lost.
- Character educators would like to see the academic work of school become more difficult and demanding, and they call for a tightening of academic standards or a return to a classical education.
- Character educators believe in creating a community within the classroom and a larger community within the school.
- Character educators exhort parents to become the moral authorities at home and join the school as partners in the character crusade.

Criticisms of Character Education

Perhaps the largest criticism of character education is the failure of its advocates to engage in empirical research. This research would not only track and document current character education efforts, it would also evaluate their effectiveness and serve as a basis for refinement of existing programs or reconfiguration of the goals of character education itself.

As stated earlier, the most recent large-scale empirical research was conducted in the 1920s and 1930s; the results contributed to the demise of character education for a long period of time. It is hard for educators, however, to justify expenditures on character education without proof beyond the anecdotal of its effectiveness.

My goal in this volume is to present—as objectively and fairly as possible—both theoretical and practical discussions of these significant issues. Through raising the most critical issues, providing well-rounded discussion, and explaining differing approaches to character education, I hope the reader will seek out additional literature and join the debate over character education—a debate that is likely to continue for some time.

1

Character Education and the Hard Business of Schooling: Kevin Ryan

Kevin Ryan is Director of the Center for the Advancement of Ethics and Character at Boston University, where he is also a Professor of Education. He explains the mission of the center as one that addresses the needs of schools and teacher education institutions, working to renew interest in character education. The coauthor (with Edward Wynne) of Reclaiming Our Schools: A Handbook on Teaching Character, Academics, and Discipline *(Macmillan, 1993), he has written or edited 15 books as well as more than 80 articles. A former high school English teacher, Ryan's primary academic foci are moral education and teacher education. He has received awards from the University of Helsinki, the Association of Colleges for Teacher Education, and the Association of Teacher Educators.*

Educating for character, to Kevin Ryan, is something sterling, pristine, and absolute—an enterprise that he views as nothing less than the moral obligation of schools. Despite his conviction that schools must educate for character in order to produce both moral and wise future citizens, Ryan—one of character education's most determined advocates—now fears that current applications of character education programs may fail.

Why, I ask, might current efforts perish?

In his reply, Ryan points to the cursory ways in which contemporary character education has been conceptualized and applied in schools. The path to virtue is hard, even severe, Ryan contends, and many contemporary educators have not been steeled to its difficulties. Placing his argument in careful context, Ryan enumerates the competing demands placed on schools. "Schools have many conflicting pressures," he begins, "including high academic standards, good athletic programs, drug awareness programs, and strong extracurricular activities. Then along comes character education. "How do schools solve this problem?" he asks. "Their resources are limited, and the intellectual preparation of staff is limited."

In fact, according to Ryan, current educators may be enthusiastic about the idea of educating for character but be ill equipped to deal with its complexity. "This generation of educators has not been prepared to think about character," he emphasizes. "They have not been prepared by universities, by colleges of liberal arts, by their own educations prior to college. They have not been prepared to think of education as an enterprise in which one imparts a vision of what it is to be a good person, a good citizen, a good worker, or a good parent."

Why, I ask, have teachers been prepared inadequately to enact a broader view of education? Isn't such a view part of educating for democracy—surely a priority?

Not so, Ryan replies. Instead, academic success—in the shallow sense of grades and SAT scores—has been emphasized at the cost of virtue. "Since virtue has been out of the ken of educators," he says, "they are ill equipped to grapple with issues such as moral and character education."

Ryan also indicts what he views as the negative contribution of the recent past. "We did many silly things in the '60s, '70s, and '80s," he says. "We thought Values Clarification was appropriate. We believed the schools should take a position of enlightened neutrality. We believed that if schools somehow engaged the young in gamelike activities, students would experience a therapeutic enlightening through which they would come to some greater appreciation and understanding of moral values."

Instead, these value-neutral enterprises, Ryan says, robbed teachers of their necessary moral authority in the classroom. "In essence," he adds, "teachers were told not to take a strong stand on issues. They were not to teach core values, to really explain what friendship is, to explain what is involved in being courageous, to point out what it means to be temperate. They were told not to use the school experience to help students acquire these strong virtues."

Character education also has not been aided by the widely varying definitions and understandings projected onto it by different people with varying goals, Ryan adds. What is character education? I ask. Its meaning seems to shift in an infinitely flexible way.

Ryan provides a classical answer. "The word *character*," he says, "comes from the Greek word, 'to engrave,' and it acknowledges the fact that people come into life and consciousness in a very plastic way. Character, of course, concerns itself particularly with the issues of what is right and what is wrong.

"When one forms a character, one forms both a moral sensibility and also the enduring habits by which people live their lives. Those habits include a sense of responsibility, a sense of diligence, or characteristics of self-indulgence or slovenliness. Character education tries to get the individual and the institution to be attentive to these issues."

Psychology Versus the Development of Character

The popularization of psychotherapy, the widespread acceptance of psychological concepts, and the entreé of psychological language into the American vernacular correspond directly, Ryan says, to the neutralization of teachers' moral authority. Do you believe, I ask him, that the popularization of psychological concepts could contribute to the nullification of character education? Do you see a causal relationship between the psychologization of the American character and the shunning of virtue in public schools?

To Ryan, the connection is sharply drawn and bleakly visible. "I look upon psychology," he responds, "as one of the major culprits in contributing to our current state as a society, although much of my own education is in psychology. As educators, we have gone overboard for psychology. We have all but abandoned the traditional disciplines which have informed the practice of education. Philosophy hardly exists in teacher preparation programs. The same is true of the history of education. These disciplines have been lost in favor of an ever-increasing prominence of psychology."

Enthusiasm about psychology needs to be placed into a context that realizes how the discipline has evolved, Ryan contends. "We need to realize that psychology itself has ricocheted from Freud to Piaget to Skinner to more current therapeutic views. Granted, all of these psychological views opened doors, and certainly, the human species is elusive and complex.

"But," he continues, "we now have a sense that psychology tells it all."

Evaluating Character Education

If many character education efforts are flimsy, how do schools realize that their moral work is lacking? What information do they need to evaluate adequately their character education efforts? When do they know they are succeeding? When should they retreat and rethink their efforts? To what extent is empirical evidence necessary?

"Evaluation," Ryan responds thoughtfully, "is the soft underbelly of the character education effort. We have trained a group of school leaders in positivism. In order to make judgments, they have to look at numbers and at what is quantifiable.

"While that is important, it is very limiting. It is very difficult to measure a change in a person's character. But it is possible to get some sense of how well a program is working through looking at things such as the school's attendance record for both teachers and students. I would look for the number of discipline referrals. How many fights have there been? How many hours do students spend in service activities within and without the school? Is there vandalism?

"How many hours are spent on homework? How much homework is done? Are test scores higher?"

These indicators, Ryan believes, are easy to obtain, although he adds, "I am not as enthusiastic as some are about trying to measure the structural changes in how people think. Since character education is the missing link in education reform, the real outcomes are revealed in students' engagement with their schoolwork."

Parenting and Character

Even if all school staff unite in the pursuit of virtue and the aims of a classical education, it is unrealistic to expect children to shift toward good character if the moral authority of parents is absent, Ryan points out.

"Parents seem to be giving much less time to raising children than ever before," he observes. "Men work longer hours; women in huge numbers are working away from their children. Although this has been wonderful for many women—and wonderful for the economy—it hasn't been very good for children because fathers haven't changed their behavior. They haven't picked up the children-raising slack."

He adds, "As a society, we haven't developed a substitute for that mother who was home to help children with their homework, to help with the social problems children experienced, to monitor them, to keep them from sitting in front of television or having their boyfriend or girlfriend over for an afternoon."

The responsibility for our current predicament is not parents' alone, he believes, but should be extended to members of the therapeutic community and university professors. "Parents have been served very badly by the therapist community, the social work bureaucrats, by professors," he says. "We have given them a set of beliefs about children that center on just providing children with a warm, nurturing, supportive environment. The belief is that if we provide that, they will bloom."

Some bloom and others perish, he warns. "Some bloom into real monsters," he adds with some astringence.

The Character Education Manifesto:
An Agenda for Action

In part because of concern about the possible trivialization of the current character education movement, the Center for the Advancement of Character and Ethics at Boston University—which Ryan directs—issued a character education manifesto in the mid-1990s. This manifesto urged that character education be thought of, and used as, a central tool in education reform.

Ryan sees character education as nothing less than "a missing link" in education reform—and as the energy that propels the charter school and voucher movement. "Many, many people are dissatisfied with the schooling their children receive in public schools," he observes, "and have taken their children out of public schools. Most of these parents express concern about the moral and ethical environment in which their children were being schooled and the desire to move to a more positive climate."

One reason so much education reform fails, Ryan contends, is that it doesn't touch people's genuine concerns. He believes that character education, if applied properly, does connect to deep parental discomfort and unease about current schooling practices.

"I don't think people are really worried about their children's SAT scores," Ryan notes. "They are worried about their children's habits, about their level of persistence when faced with difficult tasks, about their sense of personal respect and sense of responsibility. They are concerned that children are not seriously engaged in anything but their own pleasures. These are the things that upset people and move them away from the education currently provided in public schools."

Another reason that character education is central to successful education reform, he says, is the potential it offers to teachers—the possibility of more productive and pleasant working environments. "Teachers are continually hassled," Ryan asserts. "They work in morally confused, morally relaxed environments. These environments do not need to be repressive, but they do need to be places where students abandon a culture in which it is acceptable to be sarcastic to each other, to put each other down, to be unfriendly.

"This negative culture makes children afraid to open up and reach out in class, or anywhere else for that matter, because of the interpersonal hostility that they see everywhere, particularly on television. They see this on TV and then come to school, thinking that's the way they are supposed to act."

Finally, character education has at its heart and core the serious work of school, Ryan says. "We must engage children in this enterprise," he emphasizes. "This is their job when they come to school. It is their responsibility to themselves, to their parents, to their schools, to do this job well. I doubt that many children come to school feeling that they have to live up to this opportunity, but they need to realize that they should make the most of it."

The Study of Virtue

A critical component of the character education manifesto is its insistence that character education should concern itself with developing virtue, not with acquiring a discrete set of correct beliefs. What is the distinction? I ask him. Why the emphasis on something as broad as virtue, rather than on what is right and what is wrong?

Once again, Ryan indicts the social ferment of the 1960s. "During the '60s," he says levelly, "there was so much argumentation about the war, about race, about society in general. Then, with Kohlberg, we had the idea that we should engage kids in complex moral dilemmas that adults can't handle, let alone children."

Ryan believes that Kohlberg's moral reasoning approach to moral education is linked inextricably with an approach that insists that children get "the right ideas" through discussion and debate of moral concepts. But this approach, which does not position the teacher as moral authority, serves students poorly, he believes.

Teachers, he says, are more comfortable with discussion than with moral authority. Clearly, Ryan does not believe this approach will further the cause of virtue.

"Teachers," he notes, "will get tremendously exercised about ecological issues or about pro- or antifeminist positions. They feel enormously free to take fringe positions. They involve the kids in talking about these issues.

"But kids don't know the basics. They don't know what friendship is all about, what self-control means, how one gains self-control. They don't understand what it means to have a balanced view toward one's country, what real patriotism means."

As a result, Ryan argues that youth values rest on a shallow—and tenuous—foundation. Clearly, the foundation established by adults without a fundamental sense of their own values can be only shaky at best. "Kids have an almost nonexistent sense of what the core words like courage and diligence truly mean," he adds.

Ryan firmly believes that both a thorough understanding of traits such as courage, diligence, and the ability to act morally upon those characteristics are mandatory. He uses an old-fashioned—but sturdy—word to describe the aims and goals of character education: virtue.

"Studying and acquiring virtue," he emphasizes, "is what character education is about. Character education is not about helping kids acquire either politically correct or politically incorrect views."

Although character education, in its current incarnation, suffers from the danger of being both misunderstood and superficially applied, Ryan urges educators to the realization that there are ways to deepen and strengthen it. None, he cautions, are easy.

"We must concern ourselves," he insists, "with the heart and mind of the child. We have to take this on as a fundamental project, because it is more important to be a person with strong character than it is to be well-known or famous.

"I like the analogy," Ryan continues, "of the student seeing himself or herself as both the artist and the work of art. He is both the sculptor and the stone. He is working on himself, trying to use his experience at school and home, to make himself a strong person who is ready for life."

He adds, "He is the architect of his own life."

This admittedly classical view of education, Ryan says, continues to be neglected by many character educators, although there is a flurry of activity and rhetoric about educating for character. Much of this activity is ignored because it does not permeate the entire life of the school or extend deep enough into students' lives and decisions.

"Students get the sense that they need to work on their bodies, either to make themselves more attractive or to become better athletes," he states. "They may work on their skills in order to get into good colleges or get well-paying jobs. But they don't take themselves seriously as persons, in the classical sense."

Although many character educators have shifted away from using the term *values* in favor of more neutral words such as *traits* or *attributes*, Ryan remains constant to virtue. "Virtue comes from a Latin word meaning strength," he says. "But it is a very hard word. And virtue is a very difficult thing to acquire."

If taken seriously, Ryan asserts, the habits of virtue translate into a safe and orderly school environment, a classroom climate where students are not cruel to each other and where mutual respect between students and teacher rules—and where students understand why it is important to act in ways that are kind and good. "We are going to make people feel welcome and respected in our class, in our school," Ryan says. "We will extend that beyond the school into the way we, as a community, exist. We will study virtue, we will write about it, we will catch ourselves when we are about to fall.

"Above all," he continues, "we will be a people of friendship."

What do habits of virtue demand from teachers? If teacher preparation isn't adequate or targeted to the development of character, what do teachers need to be able to pursue virtue in its purest forms?

Ryan believes that the rewards of teaching in a moral school, once experienced, provide sufficient motivation for most teachers. "If you are a teacher in schools and classrooms where a strong moral ethos exists, your work is much easier and happier. You are much more satisfied with the ways in which you deal with kids. You aren't continually hassled and, in turn, hassling kids. You can get down to the work."

He concludes with quiet emphasis, "Learning is not always an easy, joyful experience, but there are many more joyful moments when teachers and students can concentrate on what they are learning together."

2

The Current Condition of Character Education: James S. Leming

James S. Leming is a Professor of Education at Southern Illinois University at Carbondale. He is a member of the Board of Directors of the National Council for the Social Studies and is a past president of the Social Science Education Consortium. A former high school social studies teacher, he has also been a professor at both Ohio University and the State University of New York at Stony Brook. During his time as a high school teacher, Leming came to the realization that learning values in schools is just as important for many children as is learning the academic basics. For the past 25 years, he has been an active researcher and author in the fields of social studies education and moral/values/character education. He is the author of three books, 12 chapters in books, and numerous articles. His recent scholarship has focused on a critical analysis of the current character education movement, the evaluation of character education and service learning programs, and the place of civic virtue in citizenship education.

A lthough character education might appear to be something new on the American landscape, it is not the first time that educators have attempted to improve societal ills through deliberate programs intended to improve youth behavior through the inculcation of values or morals.

What leads character educators, I ask Leming, to believe that current efforts will succeed where previous efforts failed? Have character education efforts changed sufficiently to indicate that they will achieve the desired outcomes? Is it realistic to expect schools to change behavior without considering the forces of economics, race, ethnicity, and culture?

The similarities between the character education efforts of the 1920s and current programs, Leming points out, are multiple. "In both periods," he explains, "one sees considerable emphasis on finding models in literature and history, using ceremonies to reward children, and establishing activities in which children create stories about what it means to be an honest person, a reliable person, and the like."

The single—and crucial—qualitative distinction between the two efforts, Leming maintains, is that current programs possess a greater core awareness of the role of the hidden curriculum and the importance of school climate. "Current programs are much more aware of these factors," he says, "while the approaches of the 1920s and 1930s were teacher centered and didactic. These earlier approaches did not devote as much attention to the indirect influences on what kids learn and how they learn it."

Like previous character education efforts, contemporary programs place significant demands on teachers—without much, if any, preparation for the moral endeavor. "Character education efforts require that teachers find a place for teaching good character in school," Leming says. "But early efforts neglected to provide much guidance to teachers."

Although major, this oversight has not been corrected. "Current efforts," he explains, "also expect quite a lot from teachers without much preparation. Teachers receive little, if any, training that is specific to character education in their preservice education."

Adequate preparation before tackling issues of virtue and values is necessary, Leming believes, if character education is to succeed in its current incarnation. In addition to some understanding of the goals of character education, prospective teachers need to acquire more than a passing familiarity with appropriate, character-focused skills.

"Character education programs do need to pay attention to providing teachers with skills," Leming emphasizes. "They also need to look at and develop more consistent curricula, rather than handing teachers materials and expecting them to automatically teach character and succeed."

One key recommendation that emerged from the Hartshorne and May research of the 1920s and 1930s, Leming notes, pointed out that indirect methods of teaching character would be more beneficial than didactic, direct methods. "Current character educators," he says, "do place much more attention on cooperative work in the classroom, having teachers function as good role models, establishing a classroom climate of caring, and making sure there is consistency between classrooms—as well as consistency between teachers, students, and parents.

"This focus on indirect methods also places a much stronger emphasis on certain kinds of behavior than in the 1920s. Today's character educators do seem informed more by basic educational research and by principles of human learning."

The Diversity of Current Programs

Although current character education advocates recognize the impact of the hidden curriculum and other variables that influence student behavior, the sheer diversity of current character education programs makes it difficult—if not impossible—to generalize about their quality. Leming points out, "When we talk about how well character education works, we first need to ask: Which program?"

Although united in the pursuit of exemplary behavior, character education programs range from those that emphasize literature to those with lists of specific values to those that try to infuse their essence into the entire school curriculum. Leming outlines the distinctions between programs, saying, "Some programs deal primarily with classroom climate and interpersonal dynamics, while others are heavily literature based. Others have a list of 32 values they are trying to teach. Some focus only on four core values. Others try to infuse character education principles into the entire curriculum. Still others are obviously behavioral in nature, while some are developmental in their focus."

The programs that show the most promise, he contends, are those that combine developmental insights into how children learn with research findings about how children are socialized. "We know how cultures transmit values and behavior, and we know under which conditions children learn these values in consistent patterns," Leming points out. "We also know what kinds of families and social environments for which that process is effective and in which kinds of environments and families it isn't."

After his recent evaluation of 10 commercially available character education programs (Leming, in press), Leming notes that only 2 of the 10 tried to incorporate both developmental principles and research about socialization. "These programs obviously stand a better chance of producing the desired results," he says, "than programs which look like the programs of the 1920s."

Because of the lack of empirical current research on the effectiveness of character education programs, Leming cautions that the characteristics of good programs simply cannot be specified. Instead, educators enter the dubious realm of hypothesis and conjecture.

"We can only speculate about the characteristics of good programs," he notes. "It is logical that effective programs should include the use of clear, developmentally appropriate language and meaningful examples of moral behavior. They should take note of demands by teachers, parents, and communities that children behave in appropriate ways. Certainly, they should include positive reinforcements for good behavior and rewards for the opportunity to practice good behavior. Parents, teachers, and the entire staff of the school should serve as good models of the particular kinds of behavior they are trying to instill."

Finally, effective character education programs need to include interesting, engaging activities for kids that focus on the desired behaviors. Leming adds, "A good program will work on a number of levels."

Why Character Education?

Although the current impetus toward teaching good character, Leming says, clearly is driven by societal concerns, other forces have propelled it to a position of prominence on the national educational agenda. "The common theme for character education programs is the state of society," he states. "Most character education programs have been able to convince foundations that they should be funded by pointing out that many children today are in crisis."

But there are other reasons that character education persists. "Another rationale," Leming continues, "is that it is inconceivable that any generation would raise its children without transmitting to them certain sorts of shared values. This is known as the cultural continuity argument. If one agrees with this contention, children do not need to be in crisis. Instead, learning the mores, values, and norms of their society is seen as a natural part of development."

Another argument for character education makes student behavior the linchpin upon which high-quality teaching turns. "Some educators argue that high-quality teaching depends upon certain student behaviors. At the core of this argument is the belief that unless students behave in a certain way, schools can't function."

Are these arguments and rationales realistic? Can character education change youth behaviors? What about the context in which children learn—particularly children from poverty who have overwhelming needs? In his reply, Leming points to a continuum.

"Most character education advocates fall somewhere between those who are convinced it will succeed in changing behavior," he explains, "and those who are mild skeptics. For instance, a number of people working in character education don't believe that the program alone will turn the school around but still believe they should try to make a positive difference."

But empirical research on character education's effects is critical, he emphasizes. "We need to know what works and to what degree. That knowledge is just one part of what any educator in the curriculum field needs to know."

Elementary Versus Secondary Programs

Because teenagers are the most likely to exhibit the antisocial behaviors deplored by character educators, why do most character education programs focus solely on elementary-age children? Are there ways in which such programs can shift to accommodate adolescents?

"About 80% of current programs do focus on elementary schools," Leming responds. "Perhaps 15% are junior high or middle school programs; less than 5% are in high schools.

"This is understandable," he continues, "because the culture of elementary schools along with the culture and mindset of teachers are keyed much more toward socializing the younger child. In high school, teachers become subject matter specialists."

The structure of most conventionally organized high schools also makes it difficult to infuse character education into the curriculum. "In elementary school, the relationship between a student and his or her teacher is much more intimate than in high school," he adds. "The teacher is knowledgeable about all the child's strengths and weaknesses.

"Elementary school teachers have a different lens through which they view education. As part of their job, they include personality development and character development as a more central part of their role than do secondary teachers. Secondary teachers are more concerned with student scores on exams. Typically, they see 150 kids a day in five classes of 30 kids. Their work is much more impersonal, much more mechanistic, whereas elementary school classrooms are much more like a family."

Visiting an elementary school and then visiting a high school points up these differences in stark terms. Although elementary school classrooms are typically warm environments where children's paintings, crafts, and artwork decorate the walls—and where it is common to see teachers working with small groups of children—high schools are much more sterile, with the day's rigid schedule punctuated by bells marking the end of class periods.

Nevertheless, the fact that character education programs typically focus on elementary-age children is, Leming says, a paradox. "Character educators will justify it on the grounds that they have to lay a foundation for the big payoff later. They see this focus in elementary schools as appropriate.

"To a certain extent," he continues, "it does make sense that if one wants to shape a child's character, efforts should begin around the age of 10. Those efforts, however, should continue through high school. Educators shouldn't wait until high school to begin character education efforts because by then many of the behaviors and roles that children have developed have become so rigid that they aren't willing to change."

The Volatility of Character Education Programs

In addition, secondary-level teachers show reluctance to engage in purposeful character education efforts because they are wary of the potential for politically volatile confrontations with parents and community members. To Leming, it is clear that most character education programs will not succeed in pleasing everyone—but if appropriate representation of the community is encouraged, potential problems can be defused at the outset.

"People on the far Right frequently believe that character education in the classroom isn't didactic enough," Leming explains. "They may express concern that the values taught are approached in a quasi–Values Clarification manner in which students discuss various dilemmas. Individuals on the far Right tend to want an approach in which there is a clear moral authority, not an approach in which students learn about gay and lesbian rights, or in which they discuss situations in which it is all right to be dishonest."

However, disagreements do not need to affect a program negatively, Leming maintains. "Most school staff realize that their job security depends more on the academic performance of students and whether the school has a safe and secure environment than on if it has a controversial character education program. That is not to say that educators are not apprehensive about possible political problems, but if they are up front with the community and enlist parent participation, a program does not need to be aligned with the Left or the Right politically."

He adds thoughtfully, "If the program is done well, it will not explode. If the program contains activities that aren't very intelligent, schools usually cut the program off quickly."

The Role of Parent Participation

Although most character educators urge parental participation, how should schools approach parents who—because of pressing demands of poverty or limited proficiency in English—cannot participate as fully as other parents? Should schools soldier on without parental involvement?

"The model for how to proceed," Leming replies, "can be found in inner-city Catholic schools. I've visited very destitute Catholic schools in urban environments, housed in disadvantaged neighborhoods. They have created small communities which contain many of the elements found in a family full of caring and warmth. School staff place high demands on students; they hold high behavioral expectations. Students are highly committed to the school."

In public schools in similar environments, Leming sees a totally different ethos. "I consulted on character education in Catholic and public schools in the South Bronx," he recollects. "In the public schools, the atmosphere was similar to army camps. Teachers' attitudes were more cavalier. Kids' behaviors were more erratic and unsupervised. High expectations and demands on students simply weren't present."

Rather than a strict emphasis on character education in impoverished, disadvantaged school environments, educators and the public have a responsibility to restructure schools, Leming believes. "We need smaller schools. We need to restaff schools with teachers who are more committed, who are more equipped for the challenges."

Leming also believes Catholic schools, with their strong parental involvement, hold key strategies that can be carried over into public schools. "One of the ways parents get their children into Catholic schools," he observes, "is through making a commitment to the education of the child. In turn, that means that school staff reach out to parents and involve them in the life of the school. Even a minimal contribution of $5 per month from parents signifies that they are committed to the education of their children."

Assessing Character Education

Although current efforts may show more hope of success than earlier efforts, Leming is adamant that they should be subjected to nothing less than rigorous scrutiny and evaluation. "All educators," he says, "have a responsibility to see that what they are doing in schools is doing more good than harm. Character education, in that regard, is no different from any other part of the curriculum."

When introducing a new program into the curriculum means abandoning something else, evidence of success is especially critical, Leming believes. "When one is fighting for space in the curriculum, evidence is needed that goes beyond anecdotes, which is frequently what is provided by character educators. Instead, there is a pressing need for evidence that is objective and credible."

Character educators need to carefully build in an evaluative component to their programs, he argues, that proves that they result in more positive behaviors. "If we want to find a place in schools for these programs," Leming says, "we need to be able to answer questions about their effectiveness. We need to know what works and to what degree of magnitude."

He concludes, "We can make a more general moral argument that states that *all* education should make a positive contribution to the development of children—and if programs are not making that positive contribution, they should be abandoned for programs more likely to succeed."

Character Education and Its Prospects
for Success: James R. Rest

*James R. Rest is a Professor of Educational Psychology at the
University of Minnesota. Well known for his research on moral
judgment development, he worked with Lawrence Kohlberg at
Harvard University as a postdoctoral fellow. This work, Rest reports, formed the foundation for his future career, developing
into research at the University of Minnesota using the Defining
Issues Test of Moral Judgment, which is used in more than 100
research projects per year. In 1986, Rest, along with colleagues at
the University of Minnesota's Center for the Study of Ethical
Development, wrote* Moral Development: Advances in Research and Theory, *a book that integrates several hundred
studies of ethical development. He is also the coeditor (with Dar-
cia Narvâez) of* Moral Development in the Professions: Psychology and Applied Ethics *(1994), published by Lawrence
Erlbaum.*

J ames R. Rest expresses his perspective on the current character
education movement as a coupling of hope and alarm: hope
that character education will succeed in achieving its desired goals,
and alarm that it will.

Why the paradox? I ask him. Rest gently points first to his
hope for character education. "Current character education advocates," he says, "are indicating a real crisis in youth development.

"Kevin Ryan and Ed Wynne, in particular, point to the appalling criminality in American life: the assaults, rapes, and murders. These are the basics for these character educators, more basic than the niceties of learning how to participate in a democracy."

He adds, "Although there is some dispute about whether we are going downhill as rapidly as they believe, there is certainly cause for alarm. In some ways, I hope that their efforts work because we are in a perilous situation."

He carefully points out that these character educators are motivated more by a crisis view of contemporary youth and society than by an approach that emphasizes the development of moral reasoning and participation in a democracy. "These character educators," he points out, "have a very different approach than one in which one uses an internal understanding of how society works and develops a set of values and skills that work well in a democracy."

Although Rest's own work focuses more on the latter, he scrupulously points out the validity of other points of view. "We have to put out the fire," he says, "before we talk about working with an architect to develop a nicer place to live."

But he admits to qualms about the possibility that character education, in its current resurgence, will succeed. "If character educators do not produce the turnaround in the statistics and appear to have solved the problem—within a relatively short period of time—it's likely that there will be a public reaction against *all* moral education," he emphasizes. "This will leave us in a worse position than we were to begin with—and the vengeance of the public will be unleashed.

"If character education does work, the radical Right will come into much more prominence in this country. This will swing much more weight toward their dominating how the country is run. Character education, when presented as a matter of what is right and what is wrong, is popular with the radical Right."

The Evidence: Values and Behavior

Why, I ask, when previous research revealed little relationship between the values held by individuals and their subsequent behavior, do current character educators believe their efforts will succeed?

In his reply, Rest places the current character education into a political and historical context. "Character education," he says, "has been more a political concern than a research-based concern. There have not been studies that disprove the Hartshorne and May studies of the 1920s and 1930s—and those studies put character education out of business for 25 years. The researchers wanted to find the opposite, but their findings showed no link between values and behavior."

Yet contemporary character educators press onward, Rest believes, encouraged by the political climate of the country—a climate that has faith in nothing less than transformational changes in society if Americans return to some halcyon time when right versus wrong prevailed. "The belief that they will succeed with their efforts," he observes, "goes hand in hand with the swing of the country against liberalism and toward conservatism. Just as character educators think Reagan succeeded with the Communists and the economy, they believe they will succeed with character education as it is currently conceived. With the swing of the pendulum, they also lump together the failed Values Clarification movement and the dilemmas discussion approach."

Why are Values Clarification and the dilemma discussion approach—usually associated with Kohlberg—considered synonymous by many current character educators? Why are they often indicted jointly when character education advocates speak of the problems facing character education today?

Rest points again to how the perceived failure of liberalism has coincided with the agenda of character educators. "Character educators talk about both of these efforts as failed liberal programs," he notes dryly. "They view the dilemma discussion approach of Kolhberg as a series of desperate science fiction dilemmas. As a result, both approaches are out of favor, although they are quite different.

"Instead, we see William Bennett and his *Book of Virtues* on the *New York Times* bestseller list for almost a year. The current message is that all we have to do to redeem society is return to those good old values that we lost somehow along the way."

But there is a political core to this message, Rest believes, and it has disturbing, long-term repercussions. "The message also is that we were subverted by liberals before," he adds. "Now, with an emphasis on core values, we're returning to the founders of our country and their beliefs. The sentiment is that the liberals diverted us for a while, but we now are resurrecting those traditions."

The beliefs that propel contemporary character education are transparently simple, he continues. Not only do character educators insist that a resurrection of the values of the founding fathers will return Americans to a simpler, less complicated past, but they see a direct link between the right values and correct, prosocial behaviors. However, this belief system does not factor in new complexities facing Americans, such as poverty, diversity of the population, or the effects of corporate downsizing.

The Aspen Agreement, Rest says, provides a good example of the goals of character education advocates. "Josephson, who heads the Josephson Institute for Morality, invited representatives from various organizations like the Association for Moral Education and ASCD—about 30 groups in all—to go to Aspen to meet for several days. They wrote the Aspen Agreement, which stated that they were in favor of character. That character was defined in terms of five or six virtues such as honesty and hard work. The purpose was to compose a united front who would promote declarations to be signed by governors within their states and similar sorts of efforts. It was the initiation of a campaign, one that would hopefully hook into political candidates, school boards, and local politics in drumming up both moral support and money for character education."

Rest believes that the combination of large promises and high expectations—added to the political climate—could result in a big explosion that would cripple the character education movement for a long time. "There is a time bomb lying within the character education movement, just waiting to be exploded," he says. "This time bomb is the tension between the religious Right and individuals such as Ryan, Wynne, and other proponents who talk about traditional values from a secular perspective rather than a religious one."

These proponents of character education, Rest maintains, have been supported by the religious Right—but the alliance is uneasy and potentially volatile. "They have gotten their support," he says, "by talking about bringing back tradition. They have given the religious Right the idea that they will return prayer to schools. When the bomb goes off, it will come from the religious Right, who will accuse character educators of secular humanism."

The Need for Research

Solid research on character education's effectiveness, Rest suggests, is clearly necessary but not likely to be endorsed by character educators. Why hasn't there been more empirical research on character education? I ask. Don't character educators want to document and refine their efforts?

Character education, it seems, is especially vulnerable to outside forces—and research, even though much needed, can be a dangerous way of calling attention to the enterprise. "There are active reasons for not doing research," Rest says. "One reason is that once you do research, the school board in your district pays attention to the fact that you are doing something with morals or values. That is likely to cause civil war in a district.

"The other reason," he notes dryly, "is that research is rarely 100% congratulatory. If confronted with negative findings, program developers need to do something about that information."

What would a sound research program look like? I ask. What central questions should it ask?

"It takes an enormous amount of thoughtfulness," he says, "and lots of small-scaled projects to learn how to put a program together that will be effective. Otherwise, there will be a flurry of activity such as the preschool and Head Start movement in the Lyndon Johnson era. Millions of dollars were spent, but we didn't know whether it did any good or not."

Obvious parallels between Head Start and the current character education movement can be seen, Rest asserts. "There is a flurry of activity with character education. There are many national meetings, including character education conferences sponsored by the White House."

Although considerable activity and publicity accompanies the current character education movement, solid research to track different approaches and to evaluate the success of those efforts is not being done. "Research tracking systems of character education activities are not in place to gather information about what is being done and what works for whom," Rest points out. "We need research so that we know how to generalize, how to make use of activities, and how to profit from them."

Ineffective research on character education, Rest points out, asks huge questions that are impossible to answer. "Rather than ask how strong an entire chain is," he observes, "it is far better to track down the individual pieces of the chain. The most effective research strategy is one that breaks the big questions into smaller units and then tracks the immediate effects of certain experiences and interventions."

Related to research on character education, he says, is the traditional tripartite view of moral education. "This view believes there are three entities: moral reasoning, moral emotion, and behavior. The reality is much more complicated. There are cognitive and emotive linkages in all components rather than only thinking, emotion, and action."

What Is Character Education?

Although current character educators present a united front about their goals and intentions, character education in practice varies dramatically from place to place. "It is a hodgepodge," Rest says laconically. To illustrate its fragmented nature, he points to books on character education that present a multiplicity of activities, some of which conflict with each other.

"One book I am thinking of," he says, "typical of others, presents approximately 100 activities for the reader. Clearly, this is a grab bag. Some ideas may appeal to a teacher; others may not. But if someone doesn't like an activity, there are others to choose. The problem with that can be seen if one uses an analogy of a pharmacy.

"One wouldn't go into a pharmacy, admire all the pills, and then take any combination because some people like some and others like others—and one is free to choose whichever combination appeals."

Although contemporary character educators have rejected both the Values Clarification approach and Kohlberg's dilemma discussions, Rest observes that dilemmas were included in this book as possible activities—although previous discussion in the volume discounted the dilemma discussion approach. He sees this as a profound contradiction within the character education movement.

"A critically tough question for character educators—as Alan Lockwood (1993) has raised—is when they should tell kids what is right and what is wrong and when they should ask kids to figure out what is right. This is key, and it needs to be addressed by the character education movement."

Can all approaches be used by all types of schools? I ask him. Or should character educators focus their approach based on student needs? Rest believes there needs to be a fit between the types of schools using character education activities and the activities themselves. He points to differences between affluent suburbs and inner cities. "There are very tough schools where living out the day can be a question," he says, "versus places such as Scarsdale or Newton, Massachusetts, which have high school philosophy and political science classes in which students debate how the Constitution ought to be framed for the public."

4

Character Education in the Classroom: Phyllis Smith-Hansen

Phyllis Smith-Hansen teaches fifth-, sixth-, and seventh-grade students at Lansing Middle School in Lansing, New York, a semirural community close to Ithaca. She is on the Board of Directors of the Center for the 4th and 5th Rs, the character education center directed by Thomas Lickona at the State University of New York at Cortland. Her teaching has been featured in the New York Times Magazine. *She has studied issues related to values for 26 years, since she began her teaching career.*

To many educators, character education is a muddy construct. At its clearest, they see it loosely linked to ideals of good behavior: from the simple niceties of getting along with others to the dramatic reduction of criminal behavior. Others press much more ambitious goals upon it—and expect it to do nothing less than redeem contemporary American society.

To Phyllis Smith-Hansen, nothing could be more straightforward—and more absolute—than character education. Given that it seems to take on almost infinitely flexible meanings, what does it mean to you? I ask.

She begins by listing what she views as common—but mistaken—perceptions. "Character education is not an additional program," Smith-Hansen says. "It is not something that you purchase.

It is not new skills to learn. It is not something you fit into what you are already doing.

"Instead, character education is a way in which the teacher views her role as an educator in the classroom," she continues. "I intend everything in my classroom to reflect on the kind of character I want my students to show—everything from my grading policy to my discipline to the way I handle their empowerment."

Deliberate, purposeful, and sure—all of these words fit Smith-Hansen's attitudes toward the entity currently known as character education. She gives an example. "An educator called me today from Pennsylvania. She wants to visit my classroom for 2 days, observing and talking to me.

"My standard policy is never to have a visitor in my room without asking my students' permission. Since we had not had any visitors yet this year, they were surprised. They said, 'You're the teacher. Why don't you just do it if you think it's right?'

"My response to them was this: 'I'm disappointed that halfway through the year you don't know better than that. One of the ways I show respect is to treat this as your classroom. I won't invite someone in without your permission—but conversely, I demand that kind of respect from you too.' "

Character education could masquerade as an isolated set of skills, she adds, but that would be misleading. "Character education is the way I relate to my students and to the material. It is the way I involve students in the life of the classroom. It is how I develop a sense of community within my classroom."

Character Education and Teachers

Why, then, I ask, are so many teachers reluctant to engage in issues related to character, given the breadth and inclusiveness of her definition?

"We are so overburdened with expectations," she responds immediately. "In our state, each school was given a report card, which measures its standardized test scores."

She adds, "Of course, that carries great weight, and it also puts tremendous pressure on teachers. This is all regarded as 'raising the standards.'"

Smith-Hansen's opinion of this is blunt. "It is myopic," she observes. "It creates a situation where teachers are unwilling to be involved with anything that might take additional time, that might divert them from that attention to academic performance."

She adds that the use of character education according to her definition can boost academic performance, although she rapidly qualifies her point. "To me, that is secondary. It is not the reason you bring character education into your classroom, but one of the secondary effects is that the kids will interact more comfortably, more positively, and therefore their standardized test scores will be higher."

Another reason that teachers may be squeamish about character education is their concern that they are mixing the sacred with the secular, Smith-Hansen points out. "Perhaps for the first time in my 26 years of teaching, we have a subject on which faith communities and public schools agree. That's frightening to many people. We have it in our consciousness that if the church likes it, there must be something wrong with it—at least where public schools are concerned.

"I also see a lot of paranoia and suspicion. Is this religion in a different wrapping? Is this sneaking religion into the public schools?"

Moral Education's Demise
and Current Character Education

A backlog of ineffective or ill-conceived character education efforts—which coincided with failed or outmoded reforms such as the open classroom—contributes to educators' skepticism, she believes. "In the '70s," she says, "we killed ourselves with Values Clarification, which set us back about 20 years. This movement gave parents plenty of reasons to be suspicious about what they saw as the question of 'whose values?'

"It was the worst thing we ever did," she adds with vehemence. "It did nothing but confuse kids. The moral dilemmas of

Kohlberg also confused kids because they were artificial. Using artificial situations to provoke values discussions was never popular with parents.

"It created," she says, "a lot of suspicion that ethics are all situational. There certainly are teachers and parents who still have a hangover from the way values were handled in public schools in the '70s."

Discussions of Moral Dilemmas

Given Smith-Hansen's description of Kohlberg's moral dilemmas discussion approach as something artificial that went out of vogue in the 1970s, I am curious about the types of discussions she leads in her classes. Since you don't position yourself as a moral authority in the classroom, how do you discuss issues related to values with your students? I ask.

Smith-Hansen, who surprises me by describing herself as a Kohlbergian, first praises the moral dilemma discussion approach—much more so than many current character educators. "When I was first introduced to Kohlberg, his approach made total sense to me. We know that kids have to be physically capable of walking before they can run. Developing a sense of right and wrong is no different than developing speech or body movements."

As she worked with the concepts, she reports she enjoyed it. "I can listen to kids' responses now and very quickly pick up their moral level. However, one gets a more accurate picture if one uses real-life situations and not artificial ones. I always use real-life situations."

She adds, "There's never a shortage of them. It might be what my mother said to me, or I didn't get a nice birthday party. There is no shortage of drama in anyone's life. Drama, if students are willing to use it, can be very interesting in a class dilemma discussion."

However, it took time for her to progress from her early years of using Kohlberg situations verbatim. "When I was first trained, I religiously used all my Kohlbergian stories. However, I don't think Kohlberg included the teacher-pleasing potential of his moral dilemma discussion approach. That's very much stage related. Very quickly, my students could figure out what made me happy to hear.

"They would give me those answers, the answers that I liked. I saw what was happening, and it was part of my early impetus to shift to real-life situations. This happened within the first 4 or 5 years of my teaching."

Character Education and Teaching

Perhaps part of teachers' uneasiness with issues related to character stems from their view of teaching. Smith-Hansen has a pristine and dedicated view of her profession—which connects directly to her vision of character education. "I dreamed of becoming a teacher when I was in the third grade," she remembers. "I looked forward to the day when I would teach. But teaching my first year wasn't exactly what I thought it would be."

At that point, she had a professional and personal epiphany: she met Thomas Lickona, a professor at the State University of New York at Cortland. Lickona is a leader in the character education movement; Smith-Hansen has studied issues related to values with him for the past 26 years. "In those days, we talked about a just community, about the whole child, about open classrooms, about taking down the walls and throwing out the desks," she says with some amusement.

"The pendulum swings back and forth, but the central meaning of education hasn't changed. We need to create a community within our classrooms. It was important to me then, it fed me then, it feeds me all the more now.

"Today, I'm thrilled that concern for the character development of children has become widespread."

She is nurtured by her belief that teachers are beginning to accept the basic premises of her concept of character education. "What has been missing have been the type of inservices or other education that would help teachers understand it," she observes. But she sees the pendulum swinging in the direction of character with the introduction of new faculty who are interested not only in academic achievement but in virtue as well.

"At my school, we have some young, new faculty who are phenomenal, and they relate to students in a holistic way," she says. "They also have a natural inclination toward character education."

A character education committee with parents as key members is in place, she reports, and it is a first step toward including the community in a broad character education effort. "Character education, in a comprehensive sense, will never exist until the community is involved. But it is nerve-wracking for schools to get involved with parents over issues related to character."

You have studied character education for 26 years, I ask, and your school is just beginning to take the first steps toward a school-wide program? Have you been singular in your efforts for most of your teaching career? Has it been an uphill battle?

"That's correct," Smith-Hansen responds, "but it has only been in the past 5 years that society as a whole has said, 'Take a look at our kids. Something is wrong. We need more education on values. We need character education.' "

The fact that the term *character education* emerged within the past 5 years is additional evidence, she believes, that society is tilting in the direction of virtue and values for its youth. "We used to call it moral education," she points out. "Character education is the new euphemism. Of course, public education has been the source of character education since its inception."

She points to various programs with an emphasis on values with which she has worked over her teaching career. "I used a program for 10 years in the third grade, and then I wrote a transition program when I was moved to fifth grade. I always negotiated these programs with the principal, saying that I would teach whatever I was assigned to teach, but I would also like to teach this."

Eleven years ago, Smith-Hansen began to work with the QUEST Program, sponsored by the Lions' Club, when area parents began to be concerned about drug and alcohol use among youth. "This program is mandated in our school for all sixth graders. Through it, they learn life skills, how to communicate with others, how to resolve conflicts, manage their emotions, make good friendships, survive changing friendships, and resist peer pressure. They learn how to make good decisions and set goals for the future."

She is especially gratified that she can help young people begin to understand that their behavior—whatever it is—carries consequences. "It's easy to look at this program and call it character education," she reflects, "because of its focus. However, anything you do in your classroom is character education. If you're yelling at the kids, that's character education, but what are you teaching them? Obviously, that the best way to relate to students is to verbally abuse them. You are not tolerant, so you encourage them to become intolerant.

"Teachers need to understand," she emphasizes, "that every minute they are character educators. If they're conscious of that, and they want certain things from the kids, they have to model that behavior."

A Classroom Suffused With Character

How do you begin, I ask, with a new class? How do they react to a classroom suffused with character?

Before she explains what she does, Smith-Hansen introduces her student population—although one senses that Smith-Hansen's approach would remain steadfast if faced with different students. "Lansing," she explains, "is an interesting school district because it is very close to Ithaca, which is a very multicultural, small city. Because of Cornell University, it attracts a lot of diversity that normally wouldn't be found in upstate New York.

"We have land that is being developed into $300,000 to $400,000 homes, and we also have fourth- or fifth-generation rural families that have a lot of problems with poverty, who live in trailer parks or on defunct farms. We have socioeconomic extremes; we are losing our middle class."

Because the student population is primarily White, racial problems found in other communities are not apparent, but Smith-Hansen paints a far from rosy picture of other dynamics. "We have all sorts of other divisions," she adds. "We have the 'haves' versus the 'have nots.' We have classism. We have sexism. We have our own set of problems."

When she begins with her regular class of sixth graders, Smith-Hansen works to break down whatever barriers and divisions exist, striving first of all to make it easier for diverse groups of youth to understand each other. "I begin," she says, "with all sorts of games and interactions that are meant to break down barriers, make kids laugh and enjoy themselves, and get to know each other."

Although the classroom atmosphere may appear light, she is moving toward a definite goal. "Through these games," she adds, "they are learning how to listen."

Her sense of timing is carefully constructed. "Five or six weeks into the year, I begin to take teachable moments. I pick different students to do this, because I have a sense by then about which students are strong, which ones can tolerate a light that shines on them for a little while."

One game she plays—called VIP—uses a tall chair that is decorated. "A student's name is picked out of a hat, and if that person is willing to participate, he or she sits in the chair. The rest of us get to ask one open-ended question that can't be answered with a yes or a no.

"The person in the chair can always pass, can always choose not to answer. The kids are awkward in the beginning. They've never tried to get to know someone. They're never learned to ask open-ended questions. So someone might ask why the person in the chair dresses in a certain way. That can be off-putting."

Smith-Hansen inserts herself adroitly into the questioning process but is careful to keep any judgment out of her voice, body language, or words. "I might say, 'Let's think of another way you can say that. What is it that you're trying to find out about this person?' She might answer, 'He always wears turtlenecks with a belt and I want to know why.'

"That's reasonable. How about if you ask it as, 'How come you wear those long turtlenecks with a belt? Why do you like them?' instead of asking, 'Why do you dress that way?'

"All that I'm doing," she adds somewhat diffidently, "is making a teachable moment stand out, making sure that I start with students that I perceive as strong enough to engage in the process without feeling nailed."

She sees a distinct payoff by the end of the year. "I reflect their words and their behaviors back to them all year," she says, "but always give them an out. They don't have to participate. By the end of the year, they're interacting as a community, working as a partnership cooperative, and listening to each other.

"There are still kids who won't actively participate in the class," she points out. "I don't insist that they do. Sometimes, students come from homes where this is something that is just not comfortable for them. They can still get something out of the class. They watch what goes on very carefully. The only requirement is to act respectfully towards other people. In other words, you don't doodle or read or throw spit wads or draw pictures while someone else does participate."

Character Education and Reflective Practice

What about the role of reflection in your practice? I ask her. To what extent does that dominate your work? How do you incorporate it into the daily pressures of teaching?

"It's not difficult," she says. "I was raised to feel that my value as a human being is based on my qualities and not my intellect, even though I was a very bright child and skipped a grade of school. Self-reflection is part of the examined life, and the unexamined life, as the quote says, is not worth living."

But is reflection difficult for your colleagues? I persist. If not raised to certain habits of mind, is it especially trying to acquire the ability to evaluate oneself critically?

"Teachers perceive themselves in definite roles," Smith-Hansen says, "and if they see themselves as givers of knowledge, then they aren't going to be self-reflective, because they think they already are."

She continues, "It is different if teachers go into teaching and see their role as interacting with knowledge and with kids, always knowing that they are going to learn something, that there is always a new point of view, there's always that phrase that is unsaid, that a student will bring some piece to the picture that I haven't thought about."

Perhaps, she suggests, it is as fundamental as a difference between teachers who have careers and teachers who have callings. "This sounds frighteningly religious," she says, "but I don't mean it to. There is a difference such as this in any kind of job. Some people are in their jobs because they feel an overwhelming rightness about it. The meaning of their lives is contained within the work that they do. That is how I feel about my teaching."

5

A Grassroots Character Education Program: Deborah Linden

Deborah Linden is the codeveloper (with Susan O'Donnell) of a character education curriculum titled RESPECT—an acronym for its core attributes. Targeted to elementary and middle school youth, the curriculum focuses on responsibility, effort, solving problems, perseverance, empathy, confidence, and teamwork, and it has been adopted by Kalamazoo County, Michigan for use with K-6 students as a training guide. Linden currently is a teacher at Comstock North Elementary School in Kalamazoo. She holds two master's degrees, one in curriculum and instruction and one in educational leadership, along with a bachelor's in elementary education. Both Linden and O'Donnell offer training in the RESPECT program locally and nationally.

A solid, collegial friendship with another teacher not only helped Deborah Linden through her first years of teaching, it also inspired her to codevelop a grassroots character education curriculum—something she never envisioned when she began teaching in 1990. As a new teacher, Linden faced students already identified as behaviorial challenges: a combined class of fourth and fifth graders categorized as "at-risk" students. Her colleague and friend, Susan O'Donnell, taught a combined early childhood and kindergarten class.

"We clung to each other," Linden reports with disarming candor, "because we were both new teachers and new to the school. We talked a good deal about teaching, about classroom management, and about ideas."

Together, the pair took a workshop offered by staff developer Susan Kovalic and were intrigued with her approach to integrated thematic instruction. Linden and O'Donnell began to think of combining the principles of integrated thematic instruction with a more deliberate focus on character education attributes—such as initiative or caring.

"We both received training in parent education," Linden says, "and returned to do a series of parent education workshops. Meanwhile, we were starting to work with our evolving concept of character skills or traits in our classrooms.

"Frankly," she adds, "most teachers expect these sorts of things from their students—good behavior in particular—but some are much more purposeful about it than others."

Linden and O'Donnell, reinforced by parent feedback, began to question how they could develop character in their classrooms—in the desire to further responsible, empathetic children, not obedient robots. "We asked ourselves: How can we do this in a more formal way in our own classrooms? We decided that the easiest way to work with students at different levels was through literature."

At first, Linden and O'Donnell worked with the literature they were already using in their classrooms but after a period of time began to seek additional stories to illustrate and supplement their activities. The current version of their curriculum uses 35 stories, although an imaginative teacher could easily select literature of his or her own and base activities on those stories.

At what point, I ask her, did you begin to think of your efforts as character education?

"Other teachers," Linden replies, "began to see behavioral changes in our students. As a result, they began to be interested in what we were doing. We also started to think of our work as something that could be integrated schoolwide."

Rather than using the word *values*, Linden and O'Donnell studiously avoided it, preferring to speak of *traits* or *life skills*. Did you sidestep the word, I ask, because of its potential for controversy in the community and with parents?

"We found that when we did parent education workshops," Linden says, "the word came up from parents. They said that we were teaching their kids values—and they loved it. Our response was, 'We prefer to call them life skills, workplace 'know-how' skills, or citizenship skills.

"We didn't want to get into the question of whose values we were teaching," she continues. "Instead, we used the terms 'traits' and 'skills' interchangeably."

The Development of a Grassroots Program

From the glimmer of an idea conceived by two teachers, the program began to mushroom, nurtured by the continuous inquiry and discussion of both Linden and O'Donnell. When she remembers how the program evolved, Linden lights up. "The primary question was: What did we want to see in our students?" she remembers. "After asking that, we always asked: How can we use our literature to further this? How can we change the ways in which we manage our classrooms? How can we teach these life skills?"

Knowing which skills, values, or character attributes to emphasize is arbitrary to a degree, Linden acknowledges. In fact, one of the difficulties of character education is the lack of consensus on which values to teach. Typical lists of virtues range from brief statements to long lists. O'Donnell and Linden looked at these lists and pondered their own for some time, submitting each prospective trait to an informal—but relentless—battery of questions. Above all, they relied on common sense.

"We knew we wanted to begin with respect," she says. "That was basic. From respect we moved to responsibility, because if you respect someone, you probably are a responsible person."

Their initial conviction that respect was the core skill they wanted to emphasize led Linden and O'Donnell to name their program RESPECT—an acronym for the core traits they wanted to emphasize: responsibility, effort, solving problems, perseverance, empathy, confidence, and teamwork.

"We kept asking ourselves: Does this make sense? Does one trait connect to another? What do we want to emphasize? What do we want to see from our students?"

Along with the core skills in the RESPECT program, students are introduced to standards to govern their behavior. Although teachers can use the curriculum without invoking the standards, Linden believes they are useful. How do these standards, I ask, tie into the rest of the curriculum?

"The teacher may tell the students what the standards are and then describe his or her expectations of the class, as a group and as individuals. These standards, taken from Gibbs's book, *Tribes*, include truth, trust, active listening, personal best, and no put-downs. To us, these are the basics, but we do recommend that students also learn some conflict resolution skills."

Outcomes of Character Education

What outcomes did you hope to achieve? I ask. What behavioral changes, in particular, did you seek?

"We want to see kids become accountable for their actions," Linden says instantly. "We find that many times they don't feel that they are, or else they don't know what is right and what is wrong. They need to know that there are consequences for their actions. Because we believe this, accountability is one of the main goals for our program.

"Our society seems to allow anything," she continues. "There is so much pressure on children, coming from television, peers, and other places. Kids see something on TV, and the consequences for whatever action they watch do not seem real because it is on TV. As a result, they may imitate the action—completely unaware of the consequences in real life."

Linden and O'Donnell also wanted to see parents become more accountable. "We've gotten away from making parents accountable," she observes. "In our district, we are moving now to making sure that parents sign their children's report cards. This may sound like a small thing, but this ensures that there is a record that shows that parents have seen their kids' grades and know what is going on at school. They can't say later on that they have done everything for this child and just can't understand why things aren't working out."

Implementing Character Education: One Program's Process

The success of most character education programs, Linden cautions, depends on the care with which they are introduced to school staff, parents, and the community. "Programs need a knowledge base and philosophical framework to succeed," she says, "not just a loose collection of ideas. It is a good idea to set up a committee at the outset that includes school personnel, parents, students, and community members representing various agencies and businesses."

With a keen eye trained on the practical, she sees no reason why this committee cannot serve dual purposes. "This committee could be the district's leadership team, school improvement team, or a group that has come together as part of an accreditation process."

The next step is to introduce the program to the school and community, through either an informational workshop for the PTA or a series of workshops conducted throughout the community. Linden prefers the latter, because the workshops invite discussion and provide an opportunity to address any questions or concerns that may arise.

"These workshops or study groups can focus on needs, concerns, and implementation strategies," she suggests. "They provide a good opportunity to gather input from other schools that have already established their own programs. It is also a time to bring in well-known speakers on character education."

The program should offer structure and guidance to teachers, Linden believes, but also allow enough latitude for teachers to make the concepts their own. Specific lesson plans are included in the RESPECT teachers' manual. Linden and O'Donnell recommend that students are oriented to the skill under scrutiny by a quick familiarization process, in which the teacher reads a definition of the skill, followed by student brainstorming that includes their own definitions and ideas for applying the skill.

Linden and O'Donnell recommend breaking each skill into three categories: "looks like, sounds like, and feels like," she says. "For teamwork, the 'looks like' category would include people together, groups, teams, sharing materials. 'Sounds like' could be talking, not yelling; sharing ideas; and no put-downs. 'Feels like' might be closeness, feeling good, feeling happy."

After student brainstorming, the teacher introduces a piece of literature to the class, followed by student discussion that is focused on how the trait was used or not used within the story. Students are asked to think of ways in which the trait could be applied to their own lives and experiences at school or at home. Clearly, students are encouraged to think and to articulate their understandings of the skills or values under discussion.

"Next, they return to their original ideas about what the skill meant," Linden explains, "and they look at how their understanding of it has changed as a result of reading the story and discussing the trait."

The story provides the basis for a teacher-led discussion, followed by activities that emphasize writing. As a final key piece, the teachers devised what they call a "homelink"—an assignment for students to take home to do with their parents.

For example, the story of Goldilocks (see Exhibit 5.1 on p. 54) highlights responsibility and the ability to solve problems, as well as respect and empathy. Although suggested activities emphasize writing, they could focus on art, math, science, music, or physical education, depending on the story's content. Careful not to let the "homelink" end at home, students receive an assignment for homeuse with their families that, when returned to school, will be used in the classroom.

Goldilocks by Jan Brett (G. P. Putnam, 1987)

Once upon a time, there was a bear family that lived in a house in the woods. One morning, they decided to go for a walk while their porridge was cooling. While they were gone, a little girl named Goldilocks came into the house and made herself welcome. When the bears returned, they found their house a mess and Goldilocks asleep in baby bear's bed. Goldilocks was startled and ran off, never to be seen again.

DISCUSSION

Ask students how it feels when someone takes or uses something without asking. Was Goldilocks being responsible? How could she have handled things differently? How could you handle difficult situations differently? How does it feel when someone gets into your desk without asking or takes something without permission?

ACTIVITY

1. You are a bear. Write a letter to Goldilocks telling her why she wasn't responsible and how that made you feel.
2. You are Goldilocks. Write a letter to the three bears apologizing for your actions and suggesting a more responsible approach.

HOMELINK

"BEARING" up to responsibility. Students take home bear patterns. When they have done something responsible at home during the week, parents write it down on the bear pattern. At the end of the week, students return the bears to school. A display can be made with a forest background.

Source: Linden & O'Donnell (1996).

Exhibit 5.1 An Example of Character Education Curricula

Schoolwide Character Education

Emphasizing the school and the community—not just the classroom—is an integral part of their program, Linden emphasizes. Speaking practically, she views the program as integral to classrooms, not an additional task.

"This is not an add-on," she says. "This is not something extra for teachers to do. This is not something with no connection to what is already going on in the classroom.

"Instead, we want to integrate and focus on positive character traits in existing curricula. We see character education as something that is cost-effective for a district, and we believe that with community buy-in to the program, the possibilities to pair with businesses increase."

As Linden and O'Donnell's workshops expanded, they emphasized the importance of the involvement of all school staff. "We wanted the playground people, the lunchroom staff, the bus drivers to come to them," she explains, "because we believed that the kids and the adults all needed to come together with a common language. In our workshops, we wanted to show some of the aspects of that common language so that there would be consistency throughout the school."

Teachers have not resisted the program, Linden adds. Why not? I ask her. What did you do to decrease skepticism and increase enthusiasm?

Linden's answer is suffused with quiet pragmatism and a thorough understanding of the frequently conflicting demands and mandates placed upon teachers. "We always begin our workshops by emphasizing that we are not trying to add on to what teachers are already doing in their classrooms. Instead, we are trying to show them a way in which they can integrate these skills into their existing curriculum. We also emphasize how these skills will help them with classroom management, and we give them ideas for incorporating these skills into a whole schoolwide program."

Linden says that she has found that teachers are particularly receptive to the idea of improving their classroom management practices, especially when they teach children with behavioral problems. "Many teachers," she says, "are dealing with kids in a grey zone. They may not have qualified yet for special education, but they have special needs. Or they come from chaotic home environments. If a teacher needs to focus on specific behaviors, these activities can be adapted to emphasize those life skills."

Both Linden and O'Donnell were guided by their own reactions to professional staff development to inform the development of their program. "We've been trained in various programs and approaches," she says. "Some are excellent; others are gimmicky. Some will not allow you to share their materials, which can be a real problem. If teachers go to a workshop but return to zero budgets at their schools, and if teachers can't reproduce the materials, there isn't much likelihood the concepts of a program can succeed.

"We knew," she adds, "our program would have to provide materials that teachers could reproduce for their own use."

Rather than focusing on teacher-led inculcation of skills and values, Linden and O'Donnell prefer newer, livelier approaches. Linden points to cross-age tutoring as another way that students can feel responsible and also learn from each other. "We show teachers the advantages of cross-age tutoring, which we also use in our program," she adds. "Kids of different ages talk about these skills, about what it means to be responsible, about what it means to show respect, and are involved together in character-enhancing activities."

Examples of such activities might include using a newspaper in class, provided by the school. The purpose, Linden points out, of using newspapers is to provide ways for students to develop critical thinking in real-life situations.

A sample assignment, focusing on teamwork, directs students to find a picture in the newspaper that shows someone using teamwork. "We ask, Why do you think this shows teamwork?" Linden says. "Students then provide some sort of rationale. With older children, we assign an article that corresponds with the skill. With many of the activities, we encourage empathy by trying to put the kids in the place of the people in the stories. We do this from the beginning discussion and persist with this focus throughout the activities and homelink."

She adds, "One little boy moved in the district and had to attend another school. He called O'Donnell back, asking for a copy of the life skills for his new teacher. He also wondered if she could get newspapers in his new classroom."

Evaluating Character Education

How has the program been evaluated? I ask. What ongoing plans are in place to monitor progress?

"We've worked to fit our program into school improvement plans," Linden says, "which fits into state requirements. A lot of schools have a school improvement process and we work with that, showing how this provides the tools to meet those standards. What we do ties beautifully into the affective goal of the North Central Association."

Their evaluation fits into fairly standard tracking devices already in place in most schools, she points out, such as the number of behavioral referrals to the principal's office and both teacher and student absenteeism. Linden believes in asking students directly about the climate of their school.

"We do student surveys all the way down to kindergarten," she says, "focusing on school climate. We do a pre-survey and then, after a year of the program, look at surveys to see if there are attitudinal changes that have occurred.

"These surveys ask, Do you feel safe at school? Is the school neat and clean? Do you feel safe using the bathroom? Are the adults in the school friendly?

"With younger children, the teacher reads the question to them and numbers the responses. All they have to do is put a check in the box that fits for them."

Over time, Linden predicts the results will inform the refinement and future direction of the RESPECT program. Clearly, she expects positive results. "Currently, many schools have only worked with this program for a year or two. If we can track students over time, it will be fascinating to see what happens."

But even to someone keenly interested in empirical evaluation of programmatic effectiveness, sometimes personal observations are just as satisfying.

"I remember one class discussion in particular," Linden says, "when we were talking about being responsible. One fifth-grade boy said, 'Ms. Linden! I was responsible this weekend!' He was quite excited about it."

The boy reported that he had been in an apartment building with some friends who were running up and down the halls, ringing doorbells at random. "He said," Linden remembers with some amusement, "that he was responsible because he didn't ring one doorbell. For him, that was one small step. Plus, he had identified the right from the wrong to a degree.

"I asked how it felt to him not to ring the doorbells, and he replied that he felt good because he knew he would get in trouble eventually if he did ring a doorbell. This showed he was thinking about consequences, and he was able to resist peer pressure."

Is Character Education the Answer?

Although Linden is the codeveloper of a character education program, she is far from a zealot convinced that character education will solve the ills of society. In fact, she places herself midway on a continuum of people convinced that character education is the answer for the woes of modern schooling and skeptics who see little benefit. "We go to many conferences on character education," she says, "and we have seen people who have such a conviction about it that they can't be objective. We, on the other hand, are realists.

"We have seen that character education has become trendy, and we know that we have to guard against that and also against doing it in a way that turns kids off. It easily could become something that kids ignore as just one more way in which teachers are preaching at them. I think this happens more when the emphasis on character is a pull-out, 20-minute session. Kids simply sit back and wait for the time to pass."

Linden also believes that successful programs need to be flexible to accommodate local needs. "Teachers need a framework," she reflects, "but they are also the ones who need to make the decisions about what they do every day in their classrooms. Every community and every school is different. Parental support varies tremendously. Teachers need to be able to work with what they think parents will be able to accept and support."

6

Schoolwide Character Education:
James Antis

James Antis is principal of Horace Mann Elementary School in Indiana, Pennsylvania, a position he has held for the past 4 years. He has been a secondary art teacher, an assistant high school principal, and a high school principal. He is completing his doctoral work at Duquesne University in Pittsburgh and holds a master's in counseling education, also from Duquesne. Challenged by the task of evaluating and documenting the effects of character education, Antis's doctoral dissertation focuses on the work he has done at Horace Mann Elementary with the Heartwood Character Education Curriculum. Horace Mann is located in a semirural district, in a university town, and in the county seat.

"It is just as important," James Antis says boldly, "to make students good as it is to make them smart. These are two completely different things, and we need to approach both in a purposeful way."

A purposeful approach to teaching virtue—or to what Antis calls "attributes of character"—needs to become part of every school's mission, he believes. Teaching character in a deliberate and focused manner should extend beyond the classroom to embrace every aspect of the school community.

"I first noticed the importance of teaching character," he adds, "when I was a principal in a senior high school. It was important to work with the students in a positive way, to make sure that they knew that discipline had to do with what they did, not who they were. I realized that we needed to focus on making kids good in a way that ensured they could make the right judgments when they were in difficult situations."

His feelings about that experience influenced his perceptions and actions when he came to Horace Mann Elementary School as its principal 4 years ago. When Antis first arrived, he was struck by the deteriorating physical appearance of the school. Quickly, he saw these physical conditions as a metaphor for other, larger concerns.

"The appearance and condition of the building needed attention," he recollects, "and student behavior needed to change."

Although at the time, Antis wasn't aware of character education's presence, he began a schoolwide improvement program that embodied many of the goals currently espoused by character educators. "We began as a school community to address issues that we thought would make our school a better place," he remembers.

The run-down physical appearance of the building provided a tangible starting point for the improvement of the entire school, and Antis seized the opportunity to encourage improvement in student behavior. "I worked hard with our custodial staff to teach them that they were not coming to school to clean commodes and sweep floors every day," he says. "They needed to know that they were coming to improve the environment. If they could make the physical environment the best it could be, then the children's learning experience would also improve. The attitudes of the adults who work in the building all day would also improve."

All this attention to school climate, Antis believes, must be part of any character education effort. "We improved the climate and tied that to teaching character attributes, such as being responsible, showing respect for the environment, and being loyal to one's school."

As building conditions and staff morale improved, Antis decided to implement the Heartwood Character Education materials and make them a deliberate curricular focus. "Two years ago, the program was implemented on a pilot basis for half a year so that teachers could become accustomed to it," he explains. "After a teacher inservice, our teachers worked with the materials on a trial basis."

The Choice of Materials

Antis chose the Heartwood curriculum, he says, because it provided a literature-based approach that uses multicultural stories, and it also emphasizes parental involvement through a range of extension activities. Teachers tell a story chosen from a wide range of literature and then lead a class discussion intended to highlight the moral of the story. The materials include specific discussion prompts, followed by a range of suggested activities, a "wrap-up" session, and extension activities to do at home with parents and other family members. For example, an activity might feature students writing about or discussing a personal experience related to honesty.

"The stories are quality literature," Antis observes, "and the extension activities encourage follow-up discussions at home. It is important for parents to discuss these issues with their children."

For example, when one teacher focused on the attribute of courage in her classroom, one child returned later and told about her grandparents who emigrated from Europe. "This illustrated courage very nicely," Antis says, "because the grandparents left relatives and belongings to come to America. The parents and the children had an opportunity to talk about the experience of the grandparents and how they demonstrated courage as they began their new life in this country.

"Another child told about her grandmother's long and courageous battle with cancer."

Teachers reinforce desired behaviors in ways that appeal to children, although Antis is quick to point out that some of these may sound, as he puts it, "gimmicky." One approach features colored, one-inch square tags. The Heartwood symbol of a tree appears on one side, and on the other, a character attribute emphasized in the program. These tags are laminated, and a collection of each attribute is distributed to each teacher. Each month, one attribute is chosen to receive schoolwide focus.

"Any time children are 'caught' demonstrating one of the attributes of character in the cafeteria, on the playground, in the halls, they are given one of these tags as reinforcement for translating character knowledge into action," he explains.

Children who receive tags during the course of the week are recognized in their class. They report what they did to merit the tag and explain how they put that particular character attribute into action.

"We also have a newspaper produced by students under faculty sponsorship," Antis adds. "A Heartwood honor roll is published in it, just as we feature an academic honor roll."

Projects are used to integrate the concepts, he points out. In a fourth-grade classroom, as part of a project focusing on hope and love, students made pillows for people in Appalachia. Materials were donated by local businesses, and parents assisted with the project. "Students made the pillows in different shapes, quilted them, and stuffed them. We sent eight boxes to lower-income day care centers in Appalachia."

A grandparents day evolved into a "grandpersons" day because some students did not have grandparents but wanted to honor people who were important in their lives. "We have classrooms in which students keep detailed notebooks and journals about character-related experiences," Antis continues. "We have neighborhood cleanups in the spring when we tend to the grounds of our school. This teaches the children responsibility for the environment."

Cross-grade activities enlist older students to read to younger students. "We need," Antis emphasizes, "to take every opportunity to integrate these activities."

The Volatility of Character Education

Antis admits to some initial concern about the potential for public controversy about Horace Mann's character education efforts. "Outcomes-based education failed in Pennsylvania," he observes, "because it had a values component. There really isn't anything we do in schools that isn't valueladen. Once the public learns that schools are dealing with value issues, they sometimes press the panic button because many people believe that schools should not teach values. It is important that the values taught are universal in nature and not related to religion or other personal values typically taught in the home."

The failure of outcomes-based education was illustrative for Antis, who redoubled his efforts to ensure that his fledgling program would not suffer a similar fate. "To begin with, we never used the word values initially," he admits, "due to its volatility."

Instead, Antis focused on the development of character and teaching what he calls "universal attributes of character."

"I talked about the attributes we were trying to teach: respect, responsibility, courage, loyalty, justice, hope, modesty, and love. The Heartwood program emphasizes seven. We added responsibility because we thought it was important."

Preliminary discussions about the importance of teaching ethics and morals became the core of the training that teachers received, Antis says. "These discussions weren't related directly to the Heartwood program," he points out, "but instead focused on a schoolwide inservice on the concept of teaching values.

"The real learning occurred later in the year," he continues, "when teachers actually were inserviced and worked with the materials, created ideas in their teaching teams and also individually."

To what extent, I ask, were there follow-up opportunities and support for teams in which they could discuss and reflect on what they were doing in their classrooms?

"Weekly team meetings," Antis replies, "are held for the different grade-level teaching teams. Our agenda for these meetings was a standard agenda with a Heartwood component. This gave us the opportunity to discuss the initiative, what we were doing, and the possibility for teams to work together on projects."

The importance of communicating the goals of any character education effort to all constituencies is critical, Antis believes, and can diffuse possible controversy. "I took every opportunity to speak to large and small groups of parents," he recalls. "Every time

I had an opportunity to explain the initiative, I did it. It was very easy to do under the umbrella of teaching kids good character."

Parents did not resist, he reports, but welcomed what they perceived as universal values. "They realized we weren't dealing with religious issues, but we were teaching the same universal values that all parents teach their children."

As a result, Antis reports he has not experienced any political difficulty with the character education program at Horace Mann Elementary. "The superintendent and school board were supportive, which is critical to its success. But it's important to pay attention to detail, particularly how the program is presented to teachers, parents, and the community."

He adds, "Telling them about what you're doing goes a long way toward diminishing any potential for unwarranted volatility."

Desired Outcomes

What, I ask, did you hope to accomplish with a focus on character education? What changes did you seek?

Although it is important for youth to understand character concepts, Antis maintains, it is more critical for them to make the transition to the desired actions, and this is where many character education programs fall short. Convinced that the link between ethical understanding and ethical behavior was critical, Antis led a schoolwide effort that focused on these specific behaviors and the logic that underpinned the correct choice of related actions.

"We began to look for ways in which kids demonstrated what they learned. We had them write about experiences in which they have demonstrated their character-related knowledge. What does it mean to be respectful? To be responsible? How do you show courage? What does it mean to be loyal?"

As teachers and school staff began to observe examples of good character, they also began to hear evidence from parents and the broader community. "We have stories told to us about how our students demonstrated behaviors that were tied directly to our character education program—and these were especially important to us because these stories come to us unsolicited."

Implementing Character Education

When implementing any purposeful program of character education, Antis emphasizes that gaining teacher acceptance is key. "There are many things that we do in school that are value laden," he says, "whether it's the way we say something, our facial expressions, or something more explicit. We teach values all the time—whether we want to admit it or not."

Although teachers realize that, he believes that they become wary when character education is laid out as a purposeful part of the school's mission. "They can become a little fearful about how parents will react," he says.

Reassuring teachers that they have administrative support is an integral part of any character education program's success, he believes. "The building principal must support teachers, rather than leaving them with a sense that they're on their own if there is a problem."

If teachers sense that they will have inadequate support, they simply will not pursue character education in a deliberate way, he believes. However, teachers at Horace Mann have supported the program—and Antis also believes that if teachers can remember why they selected teaching as an occupation, they become much more sympathetic to the aims of character education.

"When we entered teaching, there were definite reasons why we chose the profession," Antis says. "One of those was the desire to help children decide what is right and what is wrong. Knowing that, however, teachers want to be assured that they will have support."

Although character education is less common at the secondary level, Antis does not think it needs to be limited to elementary schools—where one could argue it is part of the normal socialization process that children go through, whether or not it is called character education. "If teachers are prepared and are reassured, I think character education can also be successful at the secondary level," he says. "It could be approached through club activities, through providing leadership opportunities for students, through athletics, and through choice of course-related projects. Conflict resolution can be another way to approach character education at the secondary level."

Effectiveness of Character Education: One Study

Unlike many advocates of character education, Antis is interested in tracking and evaluating the program's effectiveness. For his doctoral dissertation, he is studying the impact of Horace Mann's program, using his school as the experimental school and using a control school without a character education program. Although he continues to analyze his data, Antis reports a positive impact at the primary level, Grades 1-3, and also at the fourth grade.

"There has not been as much impact in the fifth and sixth grades," he says, "but there definitely is a difference between the control group and the experimental school."

Antis explains the difference at the fifth and sixth grades. "At the fifth- and sixth-grade levels, the teachers believe in teaching character but considered the Heartwood materials not age appropriate for their students."

Does he agree? "Not totally," Antis replies judiciously. "I see a combination of teachers thinking the materials are not age appropriate and the maturity level of fifth- and sixth-grade students. Children at that age question things more than primary-level kids and have already developed attitudes and perceptions unlike the more impressionable primary students. They sensed that their teachers thought the materials were not age appropriate. This reinforced their thoughts that some of their activities and readings were childish."

But he is not discouraged. "When the primary-aged children reach fifth and sixth grade, I predict we will see a difference. This will require a longitudinal study. My belief is that when they have worked with these materials from the beginning, they will get new meaning from the stories and the concepts at each grade level. They will experience the morals of the stories at a different maturity level and from different perspectives than when they were younger."

Antis qualifies his hypothesis, saying, "To confirm this, we will have to do some extension of my research."

Antis embarked upon his research using more than one method of measuring the program's effectiveness. He administered selected portions of the Character Assessment Inventory, developed by James Leming, as a pretest to students prior to any instruction using the Heartwood materials. The same components were administered at the end of the test year.

"This inventory," he explains, "measures both cognitive and affective character-related learning."

Antis also devised a teacher questionnaire for use at both schools. As a supplement to the Character Assessment Inventory and the teacher questionnaire, he conducted focus groups for students and parents and administered a parent survey at the experimental school.

In addition to formal evaluation and assessment, Horace Mann Elementary believes in the importance of celebration. Antis shows his pride as he describes the year-end ritual. "Our student council," he says, "created the idea of having a Heartwood program at the end of the year. Teachers and students developed the idea in each classroom at each grade level."

The results, he says, were both impressive and touching. "Students wrote songs; they wrote and performed in plays. We put all these activities together in one afternoon as a performance for their classmates, community members, and parents."

Whatever the results of his formal evaluation and assessment of the program's effectiveness, Antis takes heart from what he has observed. "We saw a wonderful culminating activity," he concludes. "It demonstrated what our children had learned about the importance of character."

References and Selected Bibliography

References

Cunningham, C. A. (1997). *The character education page.* [On-line]. Available: Internet, http://www.neiu.edu/users/uccunnin/chared.html#intro

Hartshorne, H., & May, M. A. (1927). *Testing the knowledge of right and wrong.* Six articles [by] Hugh Hartshorne, Mark A. May, and others. Reprinted from *Religious Education,* issues of Feb., Apr., Aug., Oct., and Dec., 1926, and May, 1927. [Chicago, 1927]

Leming, J. S. (in press). Whither goes character education? *Journal of Education.*

Linden, D., & O'Donnell, S. (1996). *RESPECT: Developing lifeskills for tomorrow.* Kalamazoo, MI: Donlin Educational Services.

Lockwood, A. L. (1976). *Values education and the study of other cultures.* Washington, DC: National Education Association.

Lockwood, A. L. (1993). A letter to character educators. *Educational Leadership, 51,* 72-75.

Lockwood, A. T. (1994, Spring). Character education. *Focus in Change.*

Lockwood, A. T. (1997). *Conversations with educational leaders: Contemporary viewpoints on education in America.* Albany: State University of New York Press.

Raths, L., Harmin, M., & Simon, S. (1966). *Values and teaching.* Columbus, OH: Charles E. Merrill.

Selected Bibliography

Antis, J. (1997). *What is the effect of a character education program on the intellectual, moral and social learning of elementary-aged children?* Unpublished doctoral dissertation, Duquesne University, Pittsburgh, PA.

Bennett, W. (1993). *The book of virtues: A treasury of great moral stories.* New York: Simon & Schuster.

Doyle, D. P. (1997). Education and character: A conservative view. *Phi Delta Kappan, 78,* 440-443.

Etzioni, A. (1993). *The spirit of community: The reinvention of American society.* New York: Simon & Schuster.

Etzioni, A. (1996, May 29). Virtue should be seen, not just heard. *Education Week,* p. 40.

Gilligan, C. (1982). *In a different voice: Psychological theory and women's development.* Cambridge, MA: Harvard University Press.

Hartshorne, H., May, M. A., & Shuttleworth, F. K. (1930). *Studies in the organization of character.* New York: Macmillan.

Kilpatrick, W. (1992). *Why Johnny can't tell right from wrong.* New York: Simon & Schuster.

Kohlberg, L. (1981). *The philosophy of moral development: Essays on moral development, Vol. 1.* San Francisco: Harper & Row.

Kohn, A. (1997). How not to teach values: A critical look at character education. *Phi Delta Kappan, 78,* 428-439.

Kuhmerker, L., with Gielen, U., & Hayes, R. L. (1991). *The Kohlberg legacy for the helping professions.* Birmingham, AL: R.E.P. Books.

Leming, J. S. (1993, November). In search of effective character education. *Educational Leadership, 51,* 63-71.

Leming, J. S. (1995). Reflections on thirty years of moral education research. *Moral Education Forum, 20,* 1-9ff.

Lickona, T. (1991). *Educating for character: How our schools can teach respect and responsibility.* New York: Bantam.

Lockwood, A. L. (1975). A critical view of values clarification. *Teachers College Record, 77*(1), 35-50.

Lockwood, A. L. (1991). Character education: The ten percent solution. *Social Education, 55,* 246-248.

Lockwood, A. L. (in press). What is character education? In National Society for the Study of Education, *Yearbook on character education.* Chicago: National Society for the Study of Education.

Lockwood, A. L., & Harris, D. E. (1985). *Reasoning with democratic values: Ethical problems in United States history.* New York: Teachers College Press.

Power, C. F., Higgins, A., & Kohlberg, L. (1989). *Lawrence Kohlberg's approach to moral education.* New York: Columbia University Press.

Rest, J. R. (1986). *Moral development: Advances in research and theory* New York: Praeger.

Rest, J. R. (1995). Notes for an aspiring researcher in moral development theory & practice. *Moral Education Forum, 20,* 11-14.

Rest, J. R., & Narvâez, D. (1994). *Moral development in the professions: Psychology and applied ethics.* Hillsdale, NJ: Lawrence Erlbaum.

Ryan, K. (1995). The ten commandments of character education. *School Administrator, 52,* 18-19.

Ryan, K. (1995, May 17). Character and coffee mugs. *Education Week,* 48ff.

Ryan, K. (1996). Staff development's golden opportunity in character education. *Journal of Staff Development, 17,* 6-9.

Ryan, K., & Lickona, T. (1992). *Character development in schools and beyond* (2nd ed.). Washington, DC: Council for Research in Values and Philosophy.

Wynne, E., & Ryan, K. (1993). *Reclaiming our schools: A handbook on teaching character, academics, and discipline.* New York: Maxwell Macmillan International.

CORWIN
PRESS

The Corwin Press logo—a raven striding across an open book
—represents the happy union of courage and learning. We are a
professional-level publisher of books and journals for K–12 educators, and we are committed to creating and providing resources
that embody these qualities. Corwin's motto is "Success for All
Learners."